Summer Is Here!

D0503622

Mary Garcia

Illustrated by Shane Nagle

Summer is here!
The sky is so blue.

2

Summer is here!
There's so much to do.

Summer is here!
We go to the pool.

Summer is here!
The water is **COOL**!

8

9

Summer is here!
The sun is so **HOT**!

Summer is here!
We find a shady spot.